Girls with Fangs

Jess Naomi

Thank you
for your support

Jess
Naomi

Jess Naomi

For my God and my family. Thank you for building me into a fearless fanged girl.

For Heaven, Kat, Kristen, Alia, Sara, and all the fierce women who pushed me to be fearlessly me.

For Dr. O'Neal's poetry class. You were my first sisters in poetry and my forever friends bound by words.

Fangs a lot!

The Wolf

Jess Naomi

This is the story
Of a wolf who
Became a maiden
This is the story
Of a maiden who
Became a wolf
This is the story
Of a wolf-maiden
Who crossed mountains
Fought the hunters
Tooth and claw
And came out
smiling red
Twisting apart
Under a full moon.
This is the story
Of a wolf-maiden
Who let go of the
Change
The shift between forms
And learned to sing
To the moon
Half girl
Half wolf
Completely
Whole

-     Girls with Fangs

I will not rest
Until I have held
Shells from every
Shore.
I will not stop
Until I know if
Saltwater
Tastes the same
In every ocean.
I will not settle
For a life in
Port.

-       A pirate. 350 years too late.

Jess Naomi

I would get
Bored locked
Away in a
Tower.
Claustrophobic
In a glass coffin.
My temper is far
Too hot
To sleep among
Cold ashes.
I lack the patience
For a prince.
I would have to
be the
witch.
She knows that she
Has the power
To rewrite
The story.

-    Fairytales give us a bad name

She didn't
Need a sword
To draw
Blood.
Her smile
Was sharp
Enough.
And oh,
How the
World
Bled.

- Aphrodite

Jess Naomi

They live
By the sun.
Proud.
Powerful.
Voices that
Are heard.
They hunt
By the moon.
Hidden in
Dark corners.
Our fears
Come to life.
They have forgotten
That the moon is a
Mother
And the
She-wolves
Are her children.

-      Artemis

He was all sharp edges,
Broken glass turned inwards.
Don't get too close in his eyes
Come closer in his smile
You saw a mirror in dark looks
Your own soul reflected there.
A wildness, a sharpness,
A smile like the edge of a blade.
You left the sunlight,
To chase the glint on broken glass
Judas did it for twenty pieces of silver.
You did it for a knife blade smile.

- Guinevere and Lancelot. Even queens love bad boys

Jess Naomi

Curl your hair
Sharpen your claws
Paint your eyes with
Glitter
And color your lips
To match your
Fanged grin.
The village maiden
And the monster
In the woods
Were the same girl
When she'd finally
Had enough
Of cages.

-      A Beautiful Beast

Soft guitar notes
In night still air
Lavender detergent
Against sleep-warm
Skin.
Warm feet
Cold floor
Slow drips
Of black coffee.
Teeth click against
the mug.
Hair scraped
Into fashion.
A slash of
Blood-red
On smiling
Lips.
Gunshot heels
On tile floors.
Chin high
Eyes sharp
Teeth bared.

-      Battle Ready

Jess Naomi

The bigger a
Wolf
The more power
It has
The bigger a
Girl
The more power
It takes
To be a
Wolf
In an airbrushed
Zoo
Wolves
Were never
Designed for
Cages

- Body positive

Do not presume
To tell me where
My limits are.
I will smile and
Cross them while
You watch.

- Can't: Definition not found

Jess Naomi

The sound of
A cat's
Silent footsteps.
The air that
A fish breathes.
The beginning
Of a timeless
Mountain.
Chains of
Impossibilities
Wrapped around
Fenrir's jaws.

"Women can't..."
"Women shouldn't..."
"That's not..."
"Ladylike"
"Girly"
Ribbons as weak as
Moonlight and excuses
Wrapped around
My jaws.

- Never try to chain a wolf

History
Called her
"A beauty"
As if that was
All she was.
Her enemies
Called her
"A harlot"
As if her lovers
Were the sum
Of her.
Her boldness
Intelligence
Fire
And sword
Sharp wit,
All softened
By men with
Historical pens.
Women
Called her
Queen.

- Cleopatra

Jess Naomi

His boldness
And strength
And flashing
And roar.
His rough edges
And sharp jaws.
He is a
Lion
Bear
Wolf
Eagle
Warrior
She is a
Tigress
Black Widow
Viper
She-wolf
Queen.
After all,
It's the
Lionesses
That do the
Killing.

-    Men are strong but women are deadly

I thought
I wanted
A knight
Until I realized
That no one
Fought half
As well as
A queen

-     I fight for myself, thx

Jess Naomi

I thought
I wanted
A soulmate
Until I realized
That no one
Loved half
So well as
A poet.

-    I love myself, thx

I swirl my cup
And watch the
Amber dance,
Rearranging the
Tea leaves
Into a pattern
I approve.
I trace the lines
Of my palms
With black ink,
Then draw
New ones.
I count the
Blackbirds
And forget
The number.
I toss the
Runestones
And nudge
The table.
I am not
Destined.

-    Defy the Stars

Jess Naomi

I grew up
Alongside huntresses
Warriors
Girls with blood
In their eyes
And glass
In their smile.
I never met a damsel
Who sang amongst
the flowers and
made friend with bunnies.
The only flowers I knew
Were braided in the golden hair
Of the Queen of the Underworld
And the only animals I saw
Were the stags and wolves
That raced with
The huntress.

-    You and I read different stories

Teenagers sit in a
Coffee shop and
Discuss politics.
The barista wears a button
From a protest that
Shouldn't have to happen.
A man stares out the
Rain streaked window,
Laptop flashing a news site
Filled to the brim with blood
And hate.
We sip our coffee
And wonder when stories
Became truth.

-    Life in dystopia

Head held high
Back straight
Face and heart
And soul
Bared.
Unadorned
And
Unafraid.
A Queen
Of her
Own
Making.

-     Queen Esther

Some girls
Are born
With fangs.
They file them down
To maiden smiles,
Softer and not
Quite so real.
Better for
public consumption.
But the girl inside
Still howls
When the moon is full
And the world is cold.
She breaks her teeth
To jagged points
Gnawing on chains
The world tried
to hold her with.

-      The world is afraid of the she-wolf

Jess Naomi

Dig in your claws
And bare your teeth, girl.
A wolf may be docile,
But never tamed.

-       Feminine does not mean weak

We took
The things
You used to
Hurt us
And made
Them ours.
Salt in our
Tears
Ashes round our
Eyes
Iron in our
Soul.
We made weapons
From the things
You aimed at us.
You never knew
They were for your
Own protection.

-      Fey and Wild

Jess Naomi

The arena echoes
With the cries
Of those who
Wish to see me
Fail.
The lion
Circles closer.
But my claws
Are sharper and
I will not be
Prey.

-      Gladiatrix

I grew up with
The name of an outlaw
The heart of a highwayman
And the soul of a mutineer.
Your limits were never
Meant for me.

-      He called me Jesse James

A girl in
Gleaming armor
With fire on her lips
And blood on her knuckles.
A girl who
Followed a voice like
Harps and thunder.
A girl who
Clung to her faith until
Her nails broke and split
Even as the flames and smoke
Became her new raiment.
A girl who
Sang as she burned and
Showed the world that
She would not be
Forgotten.

- Joan of Arc

They call you clever
And laugh at your
Sharp tongue.
So why are they shocked
To see the maiden smile
With fangs and wink with
Amber eyes?
Their princess was
Always a grinning
Fox in a gilded
Crown.

- Kitsune

Jess Naomi

Before she was
A damsel in distress
Did she run the
Forest trails
And howl to the stars
Teeth bared
In fierce delight?
Was she
Unapologetic
Unrelenting
Unforgiving
Before the world
Told her what a girl
Should be
And wrapped her
In red?

-    Little Red was the wolf all along

Lightening splashes
Across the sky
I jump
Hot tea
Striking the
Corner of
The page.
I take a breath
And ask again.
"How do you
Make a monster?"
You smile
And answer.
"By giving a man
Exactly what
He thought
He wanted."

-      A Conversation with M. Shelley

Jess Naomi

Breakers in her veins
Saltwater on her tongue
Her galaxy soul
Infinite
Endless
Words like comets
Fall from her lips
In ribbons of white
Fire
She went to the
Edges of the seas
The border of the stars
She drowns in moonlight
Swallowing silver light
Rising
Luminous
Reborn
Give her the sky
She will shake the constellations
Give her a voice
she will shatter reality,
her crown built from the pieces

-      She was made for starlight

Wear your heels
And lipstick
Like armor.
We go to war
Everyday,
Born with
Battle in our blood.

-    A woman in a man's world

Jess Naomi

History often
Chooses the wrong
Villain.

-      Just ask Medusa

Some monsters smile at you.
Teeth bared as an invitation,
Where wolves would
give you warning.
It draws you in
That honeyed smile
Those gentle touches
Teeth that could tear skin
Hands that could snap bone
The creature hides
Deep behind the eyes
Hunting paths only it can see
It is blood
It is nature
Something leftover
From a time when beast and man
were brothers.
It is the secret fear,
That shiver down the spine
When the lights go out
And the parking lot is empty.
A predator with blunt teeth.

-      Not all monsters have claws and fangs

Jess Naomi

The late night
Aching
Cracking
Deep in your chest
Eyes washed
In silver
Lungs filled with
Stardust
As you float on
Argent waves
And breathe

- Moonsick

Darling,
You are beautiful.
You are
Smart
Brave
Kind
Unique
You.
It's ok to
Hurt
Cry
Fear
Long.
We are what they
Name battleships
And forces of nature
After.
Water in our
Tears.
Fire in our
Eyes.
Smiles made of
Starlight.
Stronger than the
Earth.
Oh so
Beautiful.

- 	Beauty is more than appearance

Jess Naomi

I left my
Red cloak
At a fork
in the trail.
My crown
Forgotten
In the brush.
I shattered
The slipper
To fashion
A weapon
For the deep
Dark wood.
I am the
Thing that
Haunts the
Night.

-       I am no one's princess

She was not
A princess
And he was
Not her knight
Though he tried
So hard
To rescue her
From the tower
He thought
She should
Be in.

-    Not a damsel in distress

Jess Naomi

Hair littered with stars,
Eyes liquid dark,
Smile sharp as
The crescent moon.

The sea
The moon
The night
All called
By the name
Of power:
She.

- Nyx, Goddess of Night

You were
My knight
But I was
Not your
Queen.

- It's tough being "one of the guys"

Jess Naomi

Take a deep breath, darling.
Without trouble,
We'd have no need
For heroes.

-      Your origin story

Born amongst
Roses and sunlight,
The darkness must
Have felt cool on
Sun burned
Thorn pricked
Skin.

-      How sweet were the seeds, Persephone?

Jess Naomi

Growing up is
Walking past your best friend
As a stranger.
Looking at old pictures
And realizing
You have no idea
How some people
Wear adulthood.
Understanding that maybe
Just maybe
Mom and Dad
Were right.
Life is tough.
But, baby,
You are tougher.

-     Peter Pan was right

Footprints
Made of
Ashes.
Eyes of
Glowing
Embers.
Smoke
Between my
Teeth
As I
Dance
Laugh
Burn.

-     A Phoenix only knows how to rise

Jess Naomi

If I growl
And bite
And snap
And claw
It's not because
I "don't know
How to take a joke"
Or the turning
Of the month.
It is none of the
Excuses you make
For yourself.

- A wolf bites when provoked

We are a new breed of mutineers
No longer stepping
to the beat of a drum,
Backed by canon fire
Our weapons are
Thoughts
Ideas
Attitudes
Voices that refuse
to be silenced
We fight the same enemies
Oppression
Prejudice
Fear
Hate
Demons who have lived
for millennia.
We are the next generation
of rebels
This is our revolution

-      Rebel scum

Jess Naomi

Tell yourself
You are beautiful.
It is the only
Compliment you will
Receive without
Expectation of repayment.

-    Self love

Fangs do not mean cruelty.
They are our defense
Against an offensive
World.

-    I wish sharp teeth weren't necessary

Jess Naomi

If I look like a lamb,
Look closer.
Behind the pink nail
Polish and floral
Skirts that match your
Image of feminine.
See the amber eyes and
Snapping teeth.
See the wolf behind
Your assumptions.

-     Wolf in sheep's clothing

Just because an arrow
Only grazed you,
Doesn't mean you
Escaped the
Poisoned tip.

-     Always speak with kindness

Jess Naomi

If all you see
When you look
At the stars
Is a bunch of
Pretty lights
And not the
Centuries of fire
And strength bright
Enough to shine from
Worlds away,
You are missing the point.

-      Kind of like when you look at women

"It's how I show
Affection"
The lie burned
On my tongue
Like the sugar
I burnt from my veins
When the world
Said that women
Had to be made
Of fire
To be strong.

-     Sugar and Spice

Jess Naomi

Don't swing a
Sword
Then cry over
Shed blood.

-    Words cut deep

Curve to curve
Pulled taut with restraint
The more curves
The more power
The more distance between
Where she began
And where her fire
Becomes known.

-       The bow has always been the weapon of women

Jess Naomi

The softest flowers
Have the sharpest thorns.
Evolution has taught us
That without them
We are plucked
And we wither.

-      Fangs and thorns serve the same purpose

Shadows
Smoke
Flames
Sharp gold eyes
And grinning canines.
I asked for a story
And Coyote laughed.
"You." he barked,
"You will do nicely."

-      A Trickster in training

Jess Naomi

A younger me
Dreamed of fairies,
Little women with
Butterfly wings and
Cobweb gowns.
An older me knows
Not to trust a
Promise made too
Easily and a smile
A little too sharp.

-     Tricksy Fae

No one
Ever underestimates
Me when I don't sign
Emails as "Jessica".

-       Perks of unisex names

Jess Naomi

I wear my
Victories in a strand
Like Viking
Treasure beads,
Clicking against
My maiden armor.
Red for first love,
Cracked and healed
With gold.
Blue for first sadness,
Threaded through
With iron.
Yellow for first true friendship,
Shining like captured
Sunlight.
Black for doubts,
Cut through with
Silver endurance.
Green for finding myself,
Glowing brightest
In the strand.
White for future battles
To be won.

-    Valkyrie

You bask in
The light
The she craves
To touch.
You say she can't take the heat.
You tell her
That she needs
The dainty silver
Chains
And the perfume
That smells like
Holy water.
It's better this way.
Crypts are disguised
As kitchens
And bedrooms.
"A Woman's Place"
Carved into the
White ash stake
You keep just below
Her breast.

You better pray that
The silver holds.
The night has always been
A woman
And you have always feared
The dark.

- Vampiress

Jess Naomi

I like
Stormy nights
Weeping spirits
Churned up grave dirt.
I like
Fanged smiles
Silver bullets
Undead shuffling steps.
I like
The dark
The macabre
The things that
Go bump in the
Night.
I am unafraid of
Monsters
That cower
Before the
Cross.
I've been taught
How to
Fight them.

- Van Helsing was a man of faith

Nature knows
A secret that humans
Have yet to learn.
Small
Soft
Pretty
Bright
Are signs of poison,
Not weakness.

-      Venomous Creatures

Jess Naomi

Look at our
Visions of the
Future.
No shining
Chrome cities,
No flying
Skateboards,
And neon clothes.
No funny robot
Sidekick.
We see a
Future of ash,
Fighting for survival,
Escaping the bottom tier,
Trying to change the world.

You saw ivory towers,
We see wastelands.

-      The Stories We Tell Ourselves

You can keep your white knights.
Give me dark knights
with something to prove.
Give me the lost
the broken
the good people
who have done bad things
Give me the sinners redeemed
Give me the imperfect
the beaten and bruised
the mortals among saints

-    I have always loved the flawed

Sing louder
Than all your
Hurts.
Let the moon
Make silver
From your
Tears.
Shake the fear
From your
Shoulders.
You were built
For strength.
Don't let the
World
Call you
Weak.

- Wolf-child

The Maiden

Jess Naomi

The Vikings
called outlaws
"wolves on
hallowed ground"
The misfits
The castaways
Those who did
Not follow.
The fearless ones.
I remember my
Time as a wolf.
Before I shed my wolf-skin
In favor of flowers.
Traded my claws
For jeweled rings
And my fangs
For rose painted smiles.
I thought that was what
Growing up meant.

-      The wolf becomes the maiden

"I want to be a vet"
You bought me books
On every animal
I loved.
"I want to be a rock star"
You waited patiently
Outside every
Guitar lesson.
"I want to be an actress"
You drove me to
Countless rehearsals
And watched every show.
"I want to be a writer"
You still read
Every poem
I write.

-    My #1 Fan

Jess Naomi

I sat in the
Corner,
A journal open
On my lap.
You sat under
The window,
The beginnings of
A blanket
On yours.
You asked
1,000
Questions.
I made up
1,000
Answers.
The blanket
Grew
Row by row.
My story
Grew
Word by word.
Both turned
Out
Beautiful.

-     My first reader

You were
My first friend,
My total opposite,
My sometimes
Antagonist.
You lived on
The field
While I lived in
Fairytales.
You had a full
Social calendar
While I lived
In dread of
The random dots
On mine.
You were
loud music
bright colors
hot trends.
I was
Vintage tees
Comic books
Poetry readings.
Who could've
Guessed we'd grow
Up to be
So similar.

-       Little Brother

Jess Naomi

I could almost
Reach them.
My tiny fingers
Stretching up to
Brush the glittering
White starlight.
You pushed me
Towards the
Constellations.
The stars could
Be mine,
You told me,
I just had to
Reach.

- "Shoot for the stars, baby girl."

We walked on
A looking glass shore
Mother and daughter
Swapping laughter
and shells.
The shell
With a hole in the top
Would make a charm
You told me.
A mermaid's treasure.
I preferred different legends.
So I shed my
Grownup
Practical
Too-old-for-fairytales
Girl-skin.
I told you stories of
Dancing maidens
With sand on their feet
And dark liquid eyes.
Shedding their skin
Until the ocean called them home.

-      Selkies have it easy

Jess Naomi

Feet apart
Back straight.
Bend the elbow
Absorb the shock.
One breath in
Seven counts.
Exhale slow.
The arrow moves
Fast enough
for both of you.
It hits the outer ring.
Good enough.
Try again tomorrow.

-      My mother called me Robin Hood

Find a friend
Who sends you stuff
Because "it reminded me
Of you".
Who knows the names
Of characters in a book
She's never read,
Simply because it's your
Favorite.
Who tells you to always
Be yourself because
"You're kinda cool that way".

-     Find a sister

Jess Naomi

We are the hopeful.
The last drips of
Magic in a dying
World.
The havens for
Impossibilities.
The final refuge
For the dreamers.

-      An Artist's Soul

Something about
The color black
Makes me want to write
poetry.
Black coffee
In a white mug
And morning silence
That smells
Like comfort.
Black nights
An old novel
Read by lamplight.
A black sweater
Like a starlet
In a French film.
A journal
Overflowing
With black ink
Words
Words
Words.

-     A journal is a lovely companion

Jess Naomi

It became the
Unspoken rule of
The lunch table.
Everyone sat in
Comfortable silence
Nose deep in books
Of varying genres.
This, I thought,
Was the definition
Of peace.

- Unofficial book club

They are the last hope
Of those long dead.
They are the immortal voices
Echoing from ancient tongues.
They hold the stories we tell
Ourselves and we know that
We are not alone.

-    Bookshop

Jess Naomi

I try on genres
Like outfits.
Fantasy in the summer,
Loose, flowing,
Soft sunlight and glowing
Childhood days.
Scifi for a night out
Flashy, sexy,
Sleek hair and
Dark shimmery makeup.
Romance for winter
Snug, cozy,
Large sweaters
And soft mittens.
Horror for fall
Dark lace, vintage dresses,
Red lips and
Sharp smiles.
My favorites
For nights in
Comfortable as
An old hoodie,
Warm as
coming home.

-       Life built by books

I grew up in
Realms of make believe,
Climbing mountains,
Scaling towers,
Inching closer to the stars,
Until I finally grasped them
And hardly stopped to
Look back.

-    Shelves full of fantasy and Sci-Fi

Jess Naomi

My body:
Stuck at a desk
Chipped-polished-nails
Clicking against
The keyboard.

My heart:
Wandering under
Ancient trees
Parting the mist and dew
As I chase the quiet
Fay song.

-    Changeling Child

Honeyed sunlight
Bubbling melody
And fizzing coffee
That tastes like summer,
Road stretching on
And on.

-      Morning commute

Jess Naomi

I count the crows on the way
Home and hope that they never
Mention me in their hayfield council.

-     One for sorrow, two for joy

The cloud moves
Slow across the sun
Trailing sunbeams
In its wake
It looks like the
Light is racing
To greet me
As I drive
Up this
Long
December
Road

- Homecoming

Jess Naomi

One day
You will be
Driving home
And it will
Click.
All those
Mistakes
You thought
You made,
Things you
Thought
You'd never
Move past,
Aching tears
And
Heartbreaks,
They don't
Matter anymore.
Toss them
Out the window
And watch
Them shatter
In the rearview.
Smile and turn
The rock'n'roll
Up louder.

-    Highway thoughts

The stones are
Spaced so far
Apart that you
Have to leap
To the next one.
The stones behind:
Childhood
High School
College
First word
First kiss
First heartbreak.
The stones ahead:
Career
Home
Family
First love
First apartment
First forever.
You focus on
The next one
Preparing for
The jump,
Never once sparing
A glance for the
Flowers along
The way.

-    The Garden Path

Jess Naomi

The closest I've been to love
Was a cup of Earl Grey
Two sugars
And a thimbleful of milk.
He smiled
Proud to remember
The details.
Remembering
How I take my tea
Does not make me love you
When every word is a knife
And every talk is
A battlefield.
You tried to tame my fire
To candlelight
And in the end
We both burned out.

-      Sometimes I almost miss him

They say look at
The benefits
Look at the stability
Look at the future
Set in stone.
I say I've seen
All that and I
Still want to
Risk it.

- Dreamer

We talked once
About dreams.
How you only get
This one beautiful life
To attempt the impossible.
You chose the safest route.
You settled for a life on earth,
Safe, secure, practical.
I was ready to risk it all
For a walk among the stars.
Be real, you said.
Be fearless, I laughed.

-      Ground Control

He explained
Reflection
Refraction
Dust and
Sunlight
Painting the sky
Red.
She shook
Her head
And watched
The dragons
Burn the
Horizon.

-    Fact vs Fantasy

Jess Naomi

He pointed out
Constellations
Explorations
Trajectory and
Lightyears.
She told him
Stories of
Men with four arms
John Carter
Dejah Thoris
And the war for Barsoom.

- Science vs. Science Fiction

I can never
Be sure if
You were my king,
Bound by duty
And expectation,
Or you were my knight,
And I let you sail
Away with no
Goodbye.

-    Isolde

Jess Naomi

I was Catherine trapped in
a parlor with Linton,
dreaming of the moors
and sipping civil tea.
He was in love.
I was not.
He saw the world
In easy numbers
Equations
Logic.
I saw mist
On the moors,
Ghosts in the attic,
And slinking black
Dogs amongst the heather.
We would never work.
I tried to teach him poetry
He tried to teach me patience.
Sometimes I wonder if
maybe he was Heathcliff.

- Linton/Heathcliff

We found
Each other
In a
Digital world.
A warrior
That needed
A mage.
But you were
So much
Better at
Solo campaigns
And I was
Abandoned
Like an
Unfinished
Side quest.

-    Player 2

Jess Naomi

It is so
Much easier
To love
Than it is
To allow
Myself
To be
Loved.

- Romance: Better on Paper

Little me
Dreamed of white dresses
Pink roses
True love's kiss.
Grown up me
Dreams of someone
To hold me when
The world weighs too much
A soft touch
A whispered promise
Love that escaped the novels.

-    Loneliness makes poets of us all.

Jess Naomi

He was your home
your heart
Warmth and light
A fire against the cold
A burning
too bright to look at
He was everything
you dreamed of
A soft smile
and a kind heart
He was the right choice
the good choice
the safe choice
But not the one you made

-      Guinevere's choice was never easy

People go to college
And find everything
From jobs to
Soulmates
Girls graduate with
Degrees and rings.
They find forever
In their college years.
All I found
Was myself

- Graduating single

Jess Naomi

I wear my armor
Red lips
Heels clicking
Like gunfire
I carry my weapons
Heart soft enough to bleed
Mind sharp enough to cut
But you,
Oh the thought of someday-you,
You disarm me
With a smile.

-     I dream of my Prince Charming

I thought that bringing
It to lunch would make
Me read it.
I thought carrying it
Would make me seem
Cultured and complete.
I thought reading it would
Make me
Love it.

- Not all books are right, just like relationships.

Jess Naomi

We never really outgrow
The things we love.
The world just doesn't
Understand hearts
That live in
Neverland.

- Growing up

Deep in a
Hole in the
Ground there
Lived
A Hobbit.

Deep in the
Pages of a
Fairy tale
Lived
A Girl.

- Growing up in far-away lands

Jess Naomi

Hold my breath
And cross the bridge
To a land where
Spirits rule
When the lights
Go out.
Peer in cracks for
Blinking soot
Watch the sky for
Paper birds
Never make a deal
That costs you
Your name.
Now, I smile at every river
I drive past.
A thank you for letting
Me cross the water
And the border of
The worlds.

-       Chihiro: You never outgrow fairytales.

I remember
When laughter
And magic
Swirled together
In my veins.
We never
Outgrow it,
That magic,
Even when we're
Too old for
Black cats
And red
Hair ribbons.
It stays with us,
Growing,
Changing,
Pulling us
Along like
Invisible strings.
It is what makes
Us smile
When we see
A black cat
A red hair ribbon
A ragged broom

- Kiki: We never outgrow magic

Jess Naomi

I think of you
Whenever I wear a hat.
Does it suit me just
Right?
Does it tell the
World what I
Want them to hear?
Does it say that
I am the practical
Eldest child
Off to seek her fortune
In a hum-drum world
Even though she left her
Heart in a world of
Shooting stars
Fire demons
Evil witches
Charming wizards
Moving castles?
I have never quite
Shaken off
That tiny
Spark
Of magic.

-    Sophie: We never outgrow adventure.

The things I learned
From you:
Never lose your spark
Inspire yourself
Beauty is found in the everyday
Magic can be simple
Never place your heart in selfish hands
Never forget those who love you
Nature is your refuge, your teacher, your friend.
The world is as wonderful as
You make it.

-     Thank you, Mr. Miyazaki

Jess Naomi

I sometimes
Dream of running
Away like the little
Girls from fairytales.
An apple in an apron pocket.
A path through the mountain heather.
Responsibilities left at the
Bottom of the hill.
Adventures lie ahead.
Then I smile and
Sip my coffee
Tasting heather on
The air as I return to work.

-    Daydreamer

Surrounded by books,
Stories I haven't been told
And characters I've yet to meet,
While I send new explorers to
Familiar lands.
There are worse ways
To live.

-      Working in a library

Jess Naomi

I live inside
A masquerade ball.
Parading in slick
Ponytails,
Sensible shoes,
And pencil skirts.
I know the steps by heart.
A customer service smile
And a friendly bubbly
Pep in my step.
A polished professional
Human.
When midnight comes
And the ball ends
The heels fly in different
Directions,
Curled hair in a spiky bun,
A cup of coffee,
And a sigh of relief.
Nailed it.

-      Every day is Halloween

The click of
Plastic gunfire
Palms skinned raw
From gravel
Red marks on
My forehead
From a cowboy hat
Pulled low
Against the sun.

Click of
High heels
On hot concrete
Nail polish
Slightly chipped
From typing
Red marks on
My nose
From designer sunglasses
Raised high
Against the sun.

-      Even outlaws grow up

Jess Naomi

Neither flora
Or fauna,
But something
Pulled together.
Shattered mosaics
Of Midas' touch.
Honey in sunshine.
Ember eyes,
Wolf's eyes,
Only seen in
Glaring light.

    -Hazel is a boring word

I am being quirky cute
When I sit in a coffee shop
(Indie, no mainstream chains)
And I sip my latte
(Lavender. Vanilla is cliché)
And I read Hemingway or Chaucer
(One of those
look-how-cultured,
look-how-smart
books that no one really reads
for pleasure)
Baggy sweaters
(New but bought to look old)
Oversized glasses
(Millennial pink frames)
Makeup creamy, pinky, soft
(Do I look like an Instagram filter yet?)
I claim, "I don't like people"
But you can follow me on
Facebook
Pinterest
Tumblr
Twitter
Snapchat
Or both of my Instagram accounts.
I choose my books like outfits.
Classics to read in public
Poetry for coffee shops
YA fantasy and romance to read
in the comfort of my bed.
Life is about appearances
Oops, I mean
I don't care
I am 100% unique
Just like every other
"I'm not like other girls"

Jess Naomi

Girl
On the internet.

- I recognize the irony

A heart caught
Somewhere between
Honeybees
And
Ravens.

- I like cute, but I love creepy

It's in the tiny details.
A strand escaping from an updo,
Chipped nail polish,
A smudge of mascara,
A scuff on the toe of a shoe.
The tiny realities that put
You at ease,
Heart sighing,
"Ah yes. She's human too."

- Beautifully imperfect

Jess Naomi

There's something
Lonely about the
Dead words smoking
Away after
"Hi, how are you?"
"Good. You?"

-     Small talk is not a great way to make friends

Summer makes me
Want to spend
Neon nights
Of rock'n'roll
forgetting
that there has to
be a sunrise.

- Lost Girl

Jess Naomi

Lost in a book
Is where I most
Often find
Myself.

-    Protagonist

I surround myself with
Sunlight
Raindrops
Coffee hot enough
To taste
And honeyed tea
Sweet enough
To burn.
I wrap myself
In words and
Fall asleep in the
Arms of a
Story.

- Home

Jess Naomi

The smell
of tea leaves
and raindrops.
The glow of
Candlelight.
Warm fur
Under one hand,
Cool paper
Under the other.
Water against
the window.
Dog snuffling
In sleep
Beside me.
The taste of
Earl Grey
And peace.

-      Happiness takes all five senses

Cold drops against
The glass,
Tapping a song
Only they know.
There's always a bit
Of magic
In mist
And rain.

-    Perfect days for paperback adventures

Jess Naomi

I was born for
Worlds unseen.
I learned to shoot
With the outlaws
And swim with
The merfolk.
I followed a light
Through snowy
Woods and
Bumped into
A lamppost.
I wandered through
The greenwood and
Had tea with
The elves.
I went to battle
On the back of
A dragon
Because no one
Said that
I couldn't.
I was the
Chosen One
Of every story.

-     The Reader

Gods and monsters
Do battle at your
Command.
History bends and curls
At your voice
And worlds unseen
Are made known.
You are the last
Of the ancients.
You wove their voices
Into your own.

-    Every story needs a storyteller

Jess Naomi

Readers know a
Special kind of
Sadness that's hard to
Explain.
They know how to be
Homesick for places that
Never existed and
Miss people who
Never lived.

-      Fernweh

A spiderweb draped
In dewdrops
Shines brighter than
A diamond necklace
Under staged lights.

-    I prefer natural beauty

Jess Naomi

It was the kind of
morning where even
the clouds are too
weary to hold
themselves aloft
so they sink to rest
in rolls of cold fog
on the earth.
Spider webs drape
the bushes
fairy beds
recently vacated.
A lone bird
soloist in the
dawn chorus.
The morning smelled like mist,
tasted like black coffee
and poetry.

-      Sometimes mornings are nice

Bare feet slapped the sand
Racing for the waves
Never quite fast enough
to catch the foam
I waded as far
into the water
as I could
Before my mother
called me back and
I stumbled onto
sand choked shore
Fingers shriveled
Salt crusting my lashes
Hair tangled with seaweed
and wayward bits of shell

-      A mermaid learning to walk

Jess Naomi

Hands submerged
in soapy water
Glass and metal
clicking together in the sink
I raise a hand to take the towel
from my shoulder
And see the lines
and ridges
of my pruned fingers
Still dripping
suds and dishwater
The life line, love line, normal creases
Laid out like
a gypsy fortune
Lost among the web of
new cracks
And fissures,
mountains and valleys
Spread across my fingertips
Marks on a pirate's map
Bubbles cling like fishscales
Caught in the light
Before I put them back
into the water
Dreaming of salt

-    A mermaid forgetting to swim

I dream in shades
Of blue
And salt.
I live in shades
Of grass
And wind.

-    Landlocked

It is the oldest
Love song
In the world.
The sea
Caught by the
Night's pale eye,
Push and pull,
A dance of
Sighing music.
Ever bound
Together,
Ever kept
Apart.
It is the oldest
Magic
We know.

-     Stories of tragic lovers

As a writer
I am supposed
To love
Autumn.
And I do.
But there is
Something about
Spring
Sun burning the
Winter from my
Bones that is
Almost like
Turning the
Page.

-    Reincarnation

Jess Naomi

I don't know the words,
But when the night shatters
With yipping howls,
I want to sing along.

-    Coyote

Born in the
Full breath of
Spring
With snow skin
And dark hair
That spoke of
Winter's chill.
But my eyes
Were the sleepy
Green of hazy
Summer mornings,
My heart at ease
In sunlight.
I dream of
Long days and
Starlit nights.
I am the
Daughter of fireflies
And wood smoke,
A child of bright
Full moons.

-    Summer Child

Jess Naomi

Comets are predictable
Timed
Scheduled
Advertised on
The local news.
Shooting stars
Are too fast to catch
Fleeting
Shocking
Rare.
That's why they
Are magic.

-    The Difference

How can something I've
Never been close to
Feel like home?
How can I breathe it in
Until I feel luminescence
Clinging to my bones?
How can I force heavy eyes
Open for few a more seconds of
Silver bliss?
How can I know peace,
Where others fear the
Night?

- Startouched

Jess Naomi

The Wolf-Maiden

Viking shieldmaidens
Were the she-wolves
Fiercely beautiful
Swords and beaded braids
Equal weights in her world.
If they could be wolf-women,
Why couldn't I?
I chose both
The maiden and
The wolf.
I braided flowers
Into my wolf-skin,
Wore my rings on
Painted claws,
And bared my fangs
In bright red smiles.

-      The wolf maiden

Jess Naomi

At the local library
I made friends with the foxes.
Aesop's villain and
Japanese tricksters
Trotted at my heels.
I read and learned
That lynxes were the
Enemy of the fox.
Lynxes that stalk
On silent feet
That close your throat
With tears
That twine around your ankles
As you stand at the front of the class
That hold your neck in iron jaws
The night you learn the
Definition of
Claustrophobia.
I hid in tangles of words
And dens of ink and paper
And waited for the lynx
To pass me by
While I shivered in russet fur

-    I learned the meaning of a foxhole

I remember
Waiting for
The day I
Woke up to
Find out I was
Different
Special
The Chosen One
Of a grand adventure.
Until I
Stopped waiting
And started writing
My own
Story.

-   I'm the hero here

Jess Naomi

My heart knows
The stories
The voices
The heroes
The battles
If only you
Will listen.

-    Modern Minstrel

I never liked forms
But Japan taught me to see
Beautiful rhythms.

- Haiku

Jess Naomi

Nothing wakes you up
like running face first
into a wall
at six in the morning.
By wall I mean
Sleeping characters
Dead poetry
And an endless
To do list
In the real world.
How can I find
The time to
Live and write?
How can I
Live
Without writing?
Can I ignore
The itch in my fingertips
The ache in my mouth
The words bubbling
Like champagne
In my veins?
Never.

-      Writing is like breathing

I think about you
Sometimes and I wonder
If you miss me as much
As I miss the simplicity
Of our days together.
I wonder if you are
Proud to know that
The adventure continues
With new faces
New voices
Captured in ink
And paper.

-    Imaginary Friend

Jess Naomi

Learn to see
The world as a
Story
And your voice
Becomes
Your pen.

- Rewrite

The fun part is,
All writers are born
To be writers.
Some are natural,
Some take practice,
But all are born with
Creation in their souls.

- You are a writer. Write.

Jess Naomi

I don't know
How to write
A love song
Or look at
Someone
Like their
Eyes hold
Galaxies.
I don't sigh
At the sound
Of a voice
Or blush at
The touch of
A hand.
I have never
Been in love.

But, oh
My Lord,
I have
Been loved.

-      Who needs a prince when you have a King.

O Holy day
When you set me free.
O glorious day
When the chains lost
Their grip on
Me.

-    Savior

I dream of love.
The kind I've
Always read about.
The kind that
Changes lives
And shakes its
Fist at the stars.
The kind of meeting
That makes the soul
Sigh and say "At last,
I've found you."
But every time
I picture my future
I am alone.
Exploring new cities
Sipping coffee in
Old cafes
Climbing hills to
Ruined castles
Reading by fairy lights
Long after moonrise.
I am alone
And whole
And happy.

-      A Dream is not a Necessity

I was determined
To be an
Artistic nomad
Until I found a place
Where I could see
Myself, a far off
Future gray haired
Me,
Being happy.

-     Putting down roots

Jess Naomi

I dreamed of
City lights
And exotic places.
I built a life
In the place
That built me.

- Small town girl

Here's to the year
That I stopped letting
The number on
My jeans
The scale
The white box labeled "Calories"
Determine my beauty.
I replaced them with
The number of
Smiles in a day
Minutes spent with friends
Miles traveled and
Memories made.
I found a new
Definition of
Beautiful.

-     The Year of Beauty

Jess Naomi

Middle-school-me
Is grinning as
Grown-up-me
Walks around
In flowers
In red lipstick
In skull earrings
In glittery nails
In combat boots
All tied together
With pink silk
And black glitter.
It feels
Good to
(Finally)
Be me.

-    Girly Goth

Some days
It's soft curls
And flowing skirts,
Flower crowns
And honeybees.
Other days
It's leather jackets
And combat boots
Dark lipstick
And grinning skulls.
On occasion
It's sleek hair
And colorful eyeshadow
Sequin clothes
And glittery nails.
All the time
It's me.

-    Patchwork Girl

Jess Naomi

Once upon a time
There was a wolf
And a girl.
The wolf spoke
Fearlessness,
Its mother tongue.
The girl spoke
Fear,
Taught to her by the world.
Somehow they learned
To communicate.

- Learning to be me

CPSIA information can be obtained
at www.ICGtesting.com
Printed in the USA
LVHW041231050520
654998LV00003B/899

9 781093 537680